Dollars and Cents

by Marilyn Deen

WITHDRAWN

3 1308 00298 98

Consultant:
Adria F. Klein, PhD
California State University, San Bernardino

CAPSTONE PRESS
a capstone imprint

THOMAS FORD MEMORIAL LIBRARY
800 CHESTNUT
WESTERN SPRINGS, IL 60558

Wonder Readers are published by Capstone Press,
1710 Roe Crest Drive, North Mankato, Minnesota 56003.
www.capstonepub.com

Copyright © 2012 by Capstone Press, a Capstone imprint. All rights reserved.
No part of this publication may be reproduced in whole or in part, or stored in a retrieval system, or transmitted
in any form or by any means, electronic, mechanical, photocopying, recording, or otherwise, without written
permission of the publisher. For information regarding permission, write to Capstone Press,
1710 Roe Crest Drive, North Mankato, Minnesota 56003.

Books published by Capstone Press are manufactured with paper
containing at least 10 percent post-consumer waste.

Library of Congress Cataloging-in-Publication Data
Deen, Marilyn.
  Dollars and cents / Marilyn Deen. — 1st ed.
    p. cm. — (Wonder readers)
  Includes index.
  Summary: "Describes and explains the concept of making purchases, including cost of items, cash payments,
and making change"—Provided by publisher.
  ISBN 978-1-4296-7915-2 (paperback)
  ISBN 978-1-4296-8630-3 (library binding)
  1. Money—Juvenile literature. 2. Purchasing—Juvenile literature. I. Title.
  HG221.5.D44 2012
  332.4—dc23   2011022019

Note to Parents and Teachers

The Wonder Readers: Mathematics series supports national mathematics
standards. These titles use text structures that support early readers, specifically
with a close photo/text match and glossary. Each book is perfectly leveled to
support the reader at the right reading level, and the topics are of high interest.
Early readers will gain success when they are presented with a book that is of
interest to them and is written at the appropriate level.

Printed in the United States of America in North Mankato, Minnesota.
102011   006405CGS12

Table of Contents

Spending Money

You spend money on things you need or things you want. Either way, you have to make sure you have enough money to pay for the things you **buy**.

The amount of money you need depends on the **price** of the thing you want to buy. Let's go shopping and find out how much money it takes to pay for a few fun treats.

Buying a Doughnut

The first stop is the bakery. You have 1 dollar. Your favorite doughnut costs 50 cents. That is less than 1 dollar. You can buy the doughnut.

You give your dollar to the **clerk**. The clerk subtracts the amount of the doughnut and gives you the money that is left over. The leftover money is called **change**. You will get back 50 cents in change.

The next stop is the grocery store. You want to buy bananas. Your dad gives you 2 dollars. The bananas are sold for 25 cents each.

A quarter is worth 25 cents. There are 4 quarters in 1 dollar. You can buy 4 bananas with 1 dollar. You have 2 dollars, so you can buy 8 bananas.

4 quarters + 4 quarters = 8 quarters

Shopping

Now you go to the thrift store. There is a **sale** on toys. The one you like costs 2 dollars. You have a 5 dollar **bill** to spend.

You give the clerk your money. She puts your toy in a box and gives you change. You have enough money left over to buy more toys.

$5.00 – $2.00 = $3.00

It's time for lunch. You decide to get a sandwich and something to drink. You will have to spend 6 dollars and 50 cents to get the food you want. You have 8 dollars. You have enough for lunch.

You give the clerk two 1 dollar bills and one 5 dollar bill. That adds up to 7 dollars. The clerk gives you 50 cents back. You have 1 dollar and 50 cents left. That's enough for a piece of pie.

Going to the Movies

After lunch, you go to see a movie.

You have 10 dollars to spend.

A ticket costs 7 dollars and 50 cents.

$10.00 - $7.50 = $2.50

You want a snack to eat while you watch the movie. You can buy popcorn for 2 dollars and 50 cents. Will you have enough money?

You have spent all your money. The movie is about to start. Time to relax and enjoy the show!

Now Try This!

Find a shopping circular from a newspaper. Using the prices from the items on sale, make up math problems for your friends to solve. For instance: If you buy a bottle of juice for $2.39, how much change will you get back if you pay with a 5 dollar bill?

Glossary

bill   a piece of paper money

buy   to pay money to get something

change   the money given back when you pay more than something costs

clerk   a salesperson in a store

price   the amount that you have to pay for something

sale   a period of time when items are sold for less than their usual price

Internet Sites

FactHound offers a safe, fun way to find
Internet sites related to this book. All
of the sites on FactHound have been
researched by our staff.

Here's all you do:

Visit *www.facthound.com*

Type in this code: 9781429686303

And go to Capstonekids.com for more
about Capstone's characters and authors.
While you're there, you can try out a
game, a recipe, or even a magic trick.

 **Super-cool stuff!** Check out projects, games and lots more at
www.capstonekids.com

3 1308 00298 9853

Index

Editorial Credits
Maryellen Gregoire, project director; Mary Lindeen, consulting editor; Gene Bentdahl, designer; Sarah Schuette, editor; Wanda Winch, media researcher; Eric Manske, production specialist

Photo Credits
Images by Capstone Studio: Karon Dubke except: Capstone Studio: TJ Thoraldson Digital Photography, 4

Word Count: **404**   Guided Reading Level: **L**   Early Intervention Level: **18**